READINESS
IS ALL

READINESS IS ALL

The Imbalance of Western Education

ROBERT COLACURCIO

Library of Congress Control Number: 2024920901
ISBN: Hardcover   979-8-3694-3118-4
               Softcover   979-8-3694-3117-7
               eBook   979-8-3694-3116-0

Print information available on the last page.

Rev. date: 10/02/2024

To order additional copies of this book, contact:
Xlibris
844-714-8691
www.Xlibris.com
Orders@Xlibris.com
862353

CONTENTS

Chapter One: The Early Years

When I graduated from St. Xavier High School in 1960, I wasn't ready for College. My Jesuit teachers were inspiring, but they also instilled in me a noxious fear of sex and almost any kind of sexual pleasure before marriage. A woman's "erogenous zones" were places fraught with danger and the nearness of mortal sin. Though I went on so many formal dance dates that I was on a first name basis with <u>two</u> florists (innumerable wrist corsages were "safer" than ones to pin one near a girl's breast! Dating was such a mixture of innocent fun and terrible temptation to touch those erogenous zones. I wouldn't. I was a very "safe" date.

My parents' modeling of the marriage bond was not endearing or enticing. Italian table talk is naturally tumultuous, but the violent verbiage had me not infrequently slipping beneath the table to hide out. So consider the decision-making process this good Catholic altar boy had to make in senior year. Frightened by the lusty allure of sex and put off by the prospect of marriage, I discovered I had a "vocation" to enter the Society of Jesus and become a celibate monk as a Jesuit priest. I felt I was ready for that.

Consider this added element: as a critical component in the what-are-you-doing-after high school equation. My brother, seven years older and a summa cum laude graduate from a Jesuit University, exercised no little influence in my decision--though it took me eleven years of monastic study and contemplation to realize how much. The question: How do I compete with my brainiac brother? Solution: within the Catholic milieu (and both my parents being college graduates) nothing tops a Jesuit priest with a PhD. My brother had already published his first book; he's now probably the world's leading authority on Nathaniel Hawthorne. No matter. He could win a Pulitzer Prize and it would not compete with my becoming a Jesuit priest with a PhD. So that's what I did. Except for not becoming a priest.

My parental and brotherly influences gave me great study habits. I was a good student, loved languages, and excelled in the "Classical Course" at St. Xavier, which featured four years of Latin and two of Greek. I applied for entry into the Society of Jesus at seventeen, was accepted, and spent the next two years of novitiate training to be ready to undertake the military-type rigors required to become ordained as a Jesuit. Note: the Head of the Society of Jesus is referred to as "the General." St. Ignatius the founder of the S.J. was a military man, and the Jesuits are known to be "the shock troops" of the Papacy. I was ready for "boot camp."

At that time, it took 14 years--if you entered out of high school--to become almost full-fledged as a Jesuit. It takes less time to become a brain surgeon! This only slightly sarcastic joke goes, "Oh yes, the Jesuits know everything but nothing else."

When I say it took 14 years to become "almost" a full-fledged Jesuit, what do I mean? After two years of novitiate training in the spiritual life of the vows (poverty, chastity and obedience), one takes those vows for the first time, and can then sign their name with the "SJ" after. The

Jesuits are known for their special devotion and <u>readiness</u> to answer the call--whatever that might be--from the Holy Father, the Pope. After ordination and a final year of theology (after the novitiate, Jesuit training is two years of intense liberal arts; three years of formal philosophy plus a second major; three years teaching usually in a Jesuit high school; three years of formal theology plus a second major, and every summer spent in studies of some kind), the Jesuit is <u>ready</u> to take final vows. That is he is ready as a candidate and must be judged qualified. Not all Jesuits are accorded this honorific of taking these final vows that mark a man's "full integration into the Jesuit community." (<u>Jesuits</u>, USA Chicago Province, summer, 2024, p. 21) Of course, it's natural to be curious about those men who are deemed <u>really</u> <u>ready</u> for this honor after 14 years (and often more) of training and those who are not. I left the Society of Jesus after 11 years, so I have no experiential idea of how this is determined on a case by case basis.

Let's just say that in my case after 11 years, I was <u>ready</u> to leave. I left amicably. My Jesuit experience had been an academic and spiritual luxury. When asked, "Why then did you leave?" the short answer is, "It stopped being real food." Hunger is visceral. Even conceptual hunger can be felt in the pit of your stomach. The questions I was asking (as a PhD candidate in philosophy) weren't even being asked, let alone answered by my Jesuit professors at Fordham. St. Ignatius in his spiritual instruction manual, <u>The Spiritual Exercises</u>, holds up the ideal of training men to become "contemplatives in action." Recall that Ignatius of Loyola lived in the first half of the 16th century when those renegade Protestants were rebelling from the Church. Ignatius realized that the Church needed men who could "pray on their feet," out and about in the hurly burly of the world, and not limited within the confines and regimen of a cloistered monastery. I experienced the hurly burly of New York City for the last six years of my stint as a Jesuit. I discovered Zen practice was more effective at achieving the goal of contemplation in action. Many other factors contributed to my spiritual hunger, and I left the Society of Jesus. I was definitely <u>ready</u> for a change, a different modus operandi while still honoring my commitment to being a contemplative in action.

Chapter Two: The Later Years

Including high school, I had been in a strict academic environment for 15 years, and I was ready for a change. I married; she turned out to be a nymphomaniac, and ran off with my best friend after 18 months of marriage. I taught high school in midtown Manhattan and at the prestigious Convent School of the Sacred Heart (Caroline Kennedy went there). I rode my bicycle to school after my new VW Beetle was stolen ten days after purchase. That inner city teaching experience nearly killed me. Talk about unreadiness! I was both over-trained and under-trained at the same time! After three years, a totally different opportunity presented itself. I went to work on a farm in upstate New Jersey.

Rocky Hollow Herb Farm was a "front" for an esoteric school following the disciplines laid down by the Russian savant, G.I. Gurdjieff. Gurdjieff taught his own brand of Sufism. There I put in two years of hard manual labor. Boy, was I ready for that change from academia. Plus, I learned sales skills as a perfume blender of essential oils. The other half of the farm was devoted to raising Arabian horses, and I shoveled a lot of horseshit. Major Gurdjieffian take-away: there are no menial jobs, only menial attitudes.

One day after my two colleagues and I returned in our step van from a four-month sales junket selling our wares at state fairs and premium gift shows, we discovered Rocky Hollow had divided into two armed camps. Our mentors in the Gurdjieffian philosophy were a husband and wife team.

Mrs. C finally had had enough of Mr. C. bedding the nubile female students. Those who sided with her barricaded themselves in the barn-like building we used for storage, packaging and distribution of our herbal products. One-quarter mile down the road, Mr. C's contingent took over the general store and horse barn area. I definitely was not ready for this. A call to my brother in Cleveland brought him to my rescue that very night and I left RHHF silently and secretly. I was ready for another change.

My younger brother was already a very successful entrepreneur. Very soon, he would own his own plane and buy his wife a Ferrari for her birthday. He had that kind of success in sales! He suggested I keep a "low profile" while living rent-free at his home. "Take my motor bike, and in the morning visit Cleveland's numerous nurseries." It seems that Cleveland's dreadful winters produce a luxurious crop of nurseries in the spring. He thought I could easily parlay my farm experience into a job at one of these nurseries. To my brother, "low profile" meant "take it easy, take it slow." Ride around in the mornings and in the afternoon we'll play golf at his club. He was a "scratch" golfer.

By a serendipitous happenstance his friend, ROTC tent buddy, and best man at his wedding, visited shortly after I arrived. Cleveland was part of his sales territory. He worked for a company headquartered in Cincinnati--my hometown--that designed and manufactured portable displays for use primarily at trade shows. He said his company needed a salesman in Michigan so, "Why not interview for the job when in Cincinnati visiting your parents." I thought, "What the hell is a PhD in philosophy doing selling trade show displays, but what the hell." So I applied and got the job on condition that I would agree to live and work in the Detroit metro area primarily. I asked, "What's the problem? Why is this a 'condition'?" Because in 1976, Detroit was labeled the "Murder Capital of America." I laughed, "Gentlemen," I told my bosses-to-be, "I lived, bicycled and rode the NYC subways for eight years. I'm quite ready to manage your business in Detroit." So, that was my first sales job for Downing Displays Inc., and they hired me on the spot. Here's the sales training I received, "Just be ready to say 'Yes' to whatever the prospect asks you. 95% of the time, we'll be able to do what they want. Perhaps 5% of the time you'll have to back pedal and apologize saying, 'I misspoke; we can't do that. I'm sorry'."

Although I entered the sales profession with a mildly (?) condescending attitude of the typical academician towards salesmen (e.g., car salesmen), it took me only two weeks to develop a healthy respect for the sales challenge and profession. I stayed with this company for 31 years! Sales proved continually challenging in unexpected ways. What I wasn't ready for was the introduction of every new technology (CB car radio, fax machines, car phones, computers (!), and finally smart phones). Every innovation the company adopted was supposed to aid and increase my sales output; what it actually did was put another buffer between me and the decision maker who signed the purchase order. I definitely was not ready and enamored of all these technological barricades. Potential customers who had always before welcomed me in for coffee and a sit down chat about what I could do for them now were too busy to have coffee. One of the many hats new tech gave them was "gatekeeper." So what I got was, "Just fax me your quote, and we'll consider it. I don't have time to visit with you." I wasn't ready or pleased with the sales game turning unpleasant like that. Nevertheless, I stuck with it partially out of loyalty to bosses and a company who made it possible for a PhD in philosophy to earn a decent living in a market place not primarily involved in the exchange of ideas.

Because my brother was a pilot, I took some flying lessons. I quit after lesson #6 on stalls. I have two rules about flying: 1) Never jump out of a perfectly good airplane and 2) never deliberately stop an airplane's engine! After my sixth lesson on stalls, I told my wife we needed to look for a new weekend hobby. Cobo Hall Convention Center in downtown Detroit regularly hosted boat shows. We went to one, ogled the yachts we'd never be able to afford, but bought instead an 18ft Chrysler "Buccaneer" sailboat. The thing that sold me was the apparent ease the sales guy near the transom suddenly made this huge beautiful spinnaker balloon up and out of a small hole in the prow. I had to have that! The salesman told us he ran a little sailing club with weekend races on the local lakes. He said he'd teach us all we'd need to know about sailing. I'd always loved boats, especially sailboats, and so I was really ready for this new adventure of sailboat racing. It took my wife and I three years before we could hoist and rig that spinnaker during a race!

They say--whoever "they" are--that the easiest sale to make is to another salesperson. I'm not so sure about that.

What I do know is that the sales profession teaches you how to just say "No" to another sales pitch. I heard it so many times, in so many unexpected ways, that I learned how to say it right up front. My wife will dilly-dally with some solicitation at the front door for ten minutes; I just say "No" "But what if..." No. "Well perhaps I could..." No. "You see our product is different..." No! What don't you understand about the word "No"? And by the way, I could have you arrested for soliciting illegally in this neighborhood.

In my experience, in both the classroom and the sales game, readiness may not be all, but without readiness, failure is a foregone conclusion.

Chapter Three: The Mature Years

After leaving the Society of Jesus, I also left the Catholic Church. As an institution, the RCC has penned too many sheep in a corral that I call "the Dualistic Matrix." Moreover, like Jacob fooling his brother Esau with a "mess of pottage" (porridge, probably), he then went on to deceive his very near-sighted, father into giving him, the younger son, the special paternal blessing--the Church has conned the faithful out of the royal feast of their rightful inheritance. Instead of an on-going, everlasting destiny as co-creative partnership with their Divine Source in the reconstitution of this and any other universe, the faithful are fed the fatuous belief that this life is a "one-time, over-and-out" experience. They are led like sheep to obediently tread a path of strict orthodoxy. Their reward is that "cotton candy amusement park" called heaven. As typically conceived, heaven cannot satisfy the conditions for eternal character development, and is finally boring. Evidence the fact that there is so much more material about hell for comedians, stand-up comics, cartoonists and filmmakers than there is about heaven. As currently conceived for faithful consumption, heaven is frankly boring.

The true nature of the human being as spirit-in-matter is destined to enjoy endless reincarnations in co-creative cooperation and partnership with All That Is manifesting its Divinity in endlessly novel and cooperatively joyful, exhilarating ways. The institutional Church doesn't offer or promote this vision; and as the late and greatest Catholic theologian of the 20th century, Karl Rahner, SJ said toward the end of his life, "If the Church does not learn how to foster and favor the mystical inclinations of its faithful, <u>it will not survive</u>." (My paraphrase)

That "mystical inclination" is the deep readiness in the depth of each individual soul to explore the "complete, yet never completed" manifestations of endless reincarnational variations of the Cosmic Theme: "All That Is manifesting endlessly as all that is." I left the Church because it didn't satisfy my hunger to participate in this vision.

So, after leaving the Society of Jesus, I lived in New York City, and my wife and I explored <u>every</u> facet of the Human Potential Movement that was in full flower at that time. Besides Zen and Gurdjieff, I studied under Oscar Ichazo, Claudio Naranjo, Pir Vilayat Khan and Ram Das. The most influential books were those by Jane Roberts (the entire Seth series), Robert Pirsig (<u>Zen and the Art of Motorcycle Maintenance</u> and especially <u>Lila</u>, and also the works of Carlos Casteneda detailing his spiritual adventures with the Mexican brujo, Don Juan.

I spent about ten years "being guided," I truly believed, to buy the books I was directed to read. Until I was ready to meet my first "root teacher." Most esoteric spiritual traditions say something to this effect: "When the student is ready, the Teacher will appear." Meeting her, I met up with what would become my spiritual home base: the spiritual technology of the Buddha as practiced by the Nyingmapa lineage from Tibet.

Earlier I mentioned the short answer for exiting the Jesuits and also the <u>institutional</u> Church--emphasizing "institutional" because I maintained, and still do, a profound devotion to Jesus of the Gospels. I left because I was searching for "food" that neither the Society of Jesus nor the RCC provided. How do you know when you're hungry and ready for a new diet? It's visceral. That's how you know. And if that hunger (searching and questions, really) is missing, forget persuading (or being persuaded) to alter a course or adopt a new path. In all of my books (24 and counting) probably 15% of the sentences in them are questions. As a teacher, I always thought questions were more important than answers. If the student (reader or adult learner) is not <u>ready</u> because they have no vital questions that gnaw like hunger in their gut, well, the most profound "answer" can fly over without even leaving a jet stream contrail. Answers come only to questions. Better questions, better answers. And superlatively good questions can lead to life changing answers (For example, see my book, <u>The Little Book of Better Questions</u>).

I was hungry for a Path of greater soul depth leading to greater spiritual depth. Truth be told, the adjustment to the non-theistic (N.B. <u>not</u> "atheistic"!) worldview of Tibetan Buddhism actuality "shivered my timbers" at first.

Here's an amusing story about my shivering unreadiness. My first Buddhist teacher was a woman, and shortly after meeting her once, she gave a weekend retreat at the lake home of a friend in Michigan. Beautiful venue, beautiful experience. At the close of Saturday (day#2), she said, "Tomorrow afternoon, I'm offering you all the opportunity to take the Bodhisattva Vow with me." I literally wet my shorts. I had spent two years--remember the novitiate--preparing to take <u>first</u> vows in the Society of Jesus. Admittedly, this was a formal lifetime commitment, and no small potatoes: but just for <u>one life</u>. While practicing at the NY zendo I had been introduced to the bodhisattva ideal. A bodhisattva is a realized (i.e. "awakened") human being who takes an <u>eternal</u> <u>vow</u> to return again and again; that is, these supremely compassionate ones take rebirth freely without any compulsion whatsoever, and they do this for <u>only one purpose</u>: to benefit the rest of us. Benefit how? To help the rest of us get free of the Dualistic Matrix, its endless cycle of suffering, death and compulsory rebirth, and finally come to realize the evolutionary ideal of enlightenment. And they take the vow to do this for how long? Until there is no more need!

This woman, after only two days, was asking me if I wanted to take an <u>eternal</u> <u>vow</u> when I had spent <u>two</u> <u>years</u> preparing to take a <u>one</u>-lifetime vow!! I definitely felt unready for this. Desperately I sought out my wife. She was sitting quietly at the end of our friend's at dock. I ran to her in near panic, and explained my wet shorts. And do you know what she said to me--almost matter-of-factly? She said, "What else are we going to do?" My bursting balloon of a mind felt both released and rocketed into celestial space. Instantly, she helped me feel ready, and we both took the bodhisattva vow the next day.

The spiritual technology of the Buddha is a highly developed methodology of mindfulness. There is no word in Tibetan for "religion." That word is a colonial, conceptual imposition. Deeply practiced and correctly understood, Tibetan Buddhism in the Nyingmapa tradition is a contemplative <u>science</u> [sic]. To verify this for yourself, I suggest tapping into the books, YouTube videos and retreats of B. Alan Wallace. To me Dr. Wallace is currently the most superlative expositor alive today able to explain why Buddhism is a contemplative science. And because he is also a trained physicist who hob knobs with the premier exponents and practioners of quantum physics, he can clearly explain the nature of Buddhism as a contemplative <u>science</u>.

So, the question (I call this question one of my "rock candy ponderables") guiding this chapter is: Are you, the reader, ready to practice a spiritual path based on empirical, testable, repeatable and personal experience? In other words, are you ready for deeper soul depth in pursuit of greater spiritual depth? Are you ready for a Path that is in no way based on faith and belief that is captured and legislated in a credo? Because in Buddhism, belief is not a requisite, and there are no creeds or credos. None. Nothing for example, comparable <u>in</u> <u>any</u> <u>way</u> to the Nicene Creed in Catholicism.

Two things surprised me that I was not ready for. That is, the Jesuits had not prepared me with questions that made me ready for these answers. Question #1: Did you know that until 553CE, the Church allowed the teaching of reincarnation? See, for example, the writings of Church Father, Origen. In 553 CE a cabal of bishops cornered the Emperor Justinian and convinced him it was in his best interest (i.e., a power play move) to outlaw the teaching on reincarnation. And so he did. So, for the past almost 2000 years, the Catholic faithful have been conditioned to believe in only one lifetime. You only live once, one life, over and out. So, as the Budweiser ad once put it, "Go for the gusto." Truth be told, this teaching restriction enhanced the legislative power of the Church authorities most of all. How so? Ask yourself: A) <u>if</u> you only live once with that eternal "fork in the road" when you die--right fork to heaven, left fork to hell--<u>then</u> who holds the keys of power? Who enforces the "orthodoxy" (literally "right belief") and legislates the sacraments as the necessary means to salvation? Versus B): If you take rebirth endlessly until enlightenment, who holds the key to power and performance excellence now? <u>You</u> <u>Do</u>!

Question #2: According to which spiritual tradition do the Founder or Leader(s) say it's not belief or faith that is required? In fact, who says it's not a good idea to take and adopt what The Founder says on faith? No, rather take what he says and test it out against your own personal experience. Good result? Let's go further. No? Then no harm, no foul. See you again later. The Catholic Church doesn't say this. It's what the Buddha says.

But I was ready to be surprised. Are you?

Chapter Four: The Imbalance in Western Pedagogy

I've spent the first three chapters writing a kind of autobiography. If I remember correctly, the expression "readiness is all" comes from one of Shakespeare's plays. I feel it has many practical applications, but I thought this theme might engage my readers' attention better if first I illustrated its meaning and applications as personally as I could.

I want now to broaden my perspective and the range of applications. First, and perhaps foremost, I want to explore the "readiness is all" theme as it applies to our educational system in the West (i.e., its pedagogy). Our western pedagogical approach to learning I am personally and deeply familiar with, having spent many years on both sides of a teacher's desk.

It is my deeply considered opinion that our western educational system is seriously flawed because woefully imbalanced. Where does this imbalance originate? Look closely at how we start our children on their life long journey as learners. We can't get them fast enough up the learning curve of language facility. Seventy-five years ago, I was learning cursive in the third grade. Pass over for the moment the grievous omission that we no longer teach cursive. Today, many privileged kids can read even before kindergarten. Get them verbal and vocal as fast as possible so that they can fit seamlessly and uninterruptedly into adult society. Paradoxically, however, I've been told that S.A.T. tests--when they are still given--had to abbreviate the length of paragraphs to adjust to today's kids' more limited attention spans.

Recently I finished a classic novel by George Eliot. <u>Middlemarch</u> is a smart, detailed look at the life and times of ordinary folks in a mid-19th century hamlet in England called Middlemarch. One chapter opened with a <u>sentence</u> that was 250 words long! I know because I re-read it for many reasons, but ended up counting the words. It made me think of Sr. Mary Virginia, my grammar school teacher I had at Guardian Angels in Mt. Washington, an eastern suburb of Cincinnati. She regularly made us diagram compound and complex sentences. This one sentence from <u>Middlemarch</u> would have filled the entire black boards not just in the front of the classroom! Our poor little dears today can't even hang with the meaning of a 150-word paragraph, let alone visualize its sentence structure for diagramming.

Our western pedagogy is woefully imbalanced because it trains the conceptual dimension of mind almost exclusively. (The fact that most readers are asking, "What other dimension is there?" makes my point.) The conceptually developed mind is highly verbal, adept at labeling and denoting demarcations and definitions. That habit of mind makes one a secure and comfortable denizen in the Dualistic Matrix. So, where's the imbalance? Practically going unnoticed and virtually orphaned is the non-conceptual dimension of mind. This is the "naturally occurring timeless and spacious awareness dimension" that cannot be defined because its limits cannot be calculated.

It cannot be measured; it can only be experienced. This dimension provides the balance lacking when the conceptual dimension is the only one that is made familiarly facile.

The naturally occurring timeless and spacious awareness dimension offers specific differences that provide the balance, because it does the following:

1) Where the A) conceptual mind prizes labels and definitions the B) non conceptual mind is ineffable and its dimensions escape definition. It also does not define. [Hereafter A) and B)]

2) A) is time bound; B) is not. The former today instinctively looks to and for "the next best thing"; it is future oriented. The latter rests quietly content and peacefully still in the spacious openness of the present moment.

3) A) is busy about many things; it even regards "multitasking" as a premium skill. B) regards multitasking as a sophisticated distraction.

4) A) is necessarily linear. B) is not.

5) A) is enamored of the concept of "perfection," an invidious and impossible ideal to achieve a state that is "over and done," with nothing left to do or add. B) challenges that fallacy with "complete, yet not completed."

6) A) is contentious because it believes in the essential separation of phenomena, and finds the separate object sooner or later <u>objection</u>able. (B) is tolerant of differences because it regards essential separation as an illusion, a mistaken

appearance and interpretation that must be overcome.

7) A) is essential for the development of the sciences and technology. B) is essential for meditation development leading to soul depth for greater spiritual depth.

8) A) adopts Michelangelo as its artistic icon. B) adopts Leonardo da Vinci. Michelangelo shunned chatting in groups over an espresso; Leonardo sought them out. Michelangelo imposed a conceptually nuclear outline to his figures. Leonardo acutely observed there are no geometrically clear lines in nature, and his figures blended like smoke (a technique called "s'fumato") into their neighboring phenomena.

9) A) conceives separation as an essential quality of essentially independent and permanently stable phenomena. B) sees through the illusion of separation that keeps us imprisoned within the Dualistic Matrix.

Now let's be clear: both (A) and (B) are essential characteristics of the human mind. Full development of both is the ideal. The problem arises because our pedagogical system in the West pays almost exclusive attention to (A), neglecting, overlooking or even disdainfully dismissing (B) outright.

Suspend disbelief, if you must, and regard my analyses above as a hypothetical thesis to be tested for evidence pro and con. Let's for example, consider civil society today from the aspect of tolerance/intolerance, and whether (A) or (B's) cultivation makes any difference regarding the tumult and turmoil we are experiencing in society today.

As I write (it's early August 2024), President Joe Biden has just decided not to run for re-election against Donald Trump. He's passed the baton to Kamala Harris. Consider, for openers, Joe's resignation speech (7-24-24). It is filled with a gracious thankfulness and joy for the privilege he enjoyed for 50 years of public service. His attitude was spaciously hopeful for the preservation of our constitutional democracy, and felt like a love letter to his devoted family, faithful team, and millions of supporters. "Tolerant" would be at best a sidebar comment, a magnificent misobservation! His demeanor, his tone, his words reflected the attitude of a job "complete, yet not completed." Trump's bellicose response was a blustery fusillade of angry attack and divisive intolerance of not only "the old sleepy Joe Biden," but the newly minted "side stepping Biden" for the good of the country foremost and his legacy not even an afterthought.

Consider the dimension of mind that each man's words were germinated and flowered from. Trump exhibited exclusively (A) characteristics: extremism, contentious division and fallacious definition that relied on conjured concepts arising out of a mind contracted even more tightly than normal. Trump was totally non plussed by the implausibility of doing something--a la George Washington--that he could only conceive as an impossibility. Biden by contrast was conceptually clear and concise. No rambling 91-minute bloviation as in Trump's RNC acceptance speech. Biden was firm but malleable in his acknowledgment of the realities expected of him. He exhibited a spacious clarity of mind and a generosity of spirit: evidence, in my opinion, that his delivery was germinated in the timeless spaciousness of the naturally occurring awareness dimension (B) of mind. As they say, the telling truly is in the tasting, and what taste did each man's remarks leave in your mouth?

Trump-Vance vs. Harris-Walz is a symbol that is symptomatic of cultural tectonic plates that have been grinding towards this tsunami for some time now.

It is my opinion that the imbalance in our pedagogy is one of the root causes that are evidenced by the unrest, belligerence, violence, hateful divisiveness and outright chaos that we are experiencing in what passes for civil society today. In the next chapter, I will develop this theme more deeply.

Chapter Five: Imbalance and the Mind of Civility

I just finished writing a book titled, <u>You Make Me So Fat: Why Be Bothered by Blaming</u>. The foolishness of the title is meant to alert the reader to the fact that while blaming another for your excessive caloric intake is fatuous (pun intended!); the reality is we most often don't take responsibility and ownership of our own feelings. For example, "You make me so mad I could...," sounds immediately plausible and even justifiable if the details of the social situation could be clearly known. Wrong. Explanation and justification are two very different things; the rationale for each is logically, psychologically and philosophically different. Observation of the human scene, even casually, shows how ready we all are to blame others for what we feel. My book (above) details why this attitude and habitual propensity is not just a mistake; it also insidiously continues to perpetuate our self-imposed imprisonment in the Dualistic Matrix, which according to the Buddha, is the source and existential context for all human suffering.

Blaming is an example of being radically off balance. Observing blaming in action, one can almost see that the "plumb line," if you will, of the person doing the blaming, is off center. How many degrees off center is for you, the reader, to observe. Recently I suffered a stroke that turned my right leg into a wet noodle. Even with the help of two burly PT assistants, I couldn't help leaning 10-15 degrees to the right, even though I felt I was standing plumb line straight. It took me several weeks in rehab before I re-established a feeling for that internal plumb line. Again, until that happened, I didn't <u>feel</u> safe getting up from my wheel chair and using a walker on my own. Lack of balance meant I wasn't ready to walk.

Paradoxically, is it the case that the quick readiness we have to say, "Oh, I'm sorry" is also an example of imbalance? A friend of mind thinks so; and she explains herself by asking me to observe how, in her view, we are schooled as children to immediately "salve" (my word, not hers) over the "disconnect" with a boiler plate-like sticker that reads, "Oh, I'm [so] sorry." I'm not exactly clear about what my friend would have us do or say instead, but her thoughts stimulated my own on his topic. Two popular sayings come to mind: 1) "Love means never having to say you're sorry," from the film <u>Love Story</u> and 2) This from the song by Elton John, "Sorry seems to be the hardest word." In both cases, I ask you, "Why?" Why would you never apologize to someone you love? To someone very near and dear to me who is suffering from the early stages of dementia, I frequently apologize that my frustration bursts out with vocal irritation and complaint. No matter that nine times out of ten, I bite my tongue and say nothing. I lost my patience on the tenth time, and loudly misspoke. "I'm sorry" is the appropriate apology. Not saying, "I'm sorry" is I feel an example of imbalance. How so? Psychologically speaking, my mental plumb line tilted by my outburst of frustration, and restoration of psychological and emotional balance requires an apology.

Regarding Elton John's "Sorry seems to be the hardest word," Why is that? My friend thinks most of us are too ready to gloss over a situation with "I'm sorry," and Elton John thinks we're too reluctant. Which is it? Probably both. Why/when is it hard to say/be sorry? Perhaps the simplest yet most profound reason is pride. And curiously (?), beneath pride is fear. According to the Buddha, fear is actually one of the two brackets that "bookend" the range of negative emotions. I'll leave it to the reader to ponder--one of those "rock candy ponderables-what emotion bookends the other end of the range or spectrum of negative emotions. (I think you'd be quite surprised by what the Buddha says it is.) In any case, being too proud to make amends with, "I'm sorry" is, I'm sorry to say, a psychological imbalance rooted ultimately in pride and fear.

Now then, since pride and fear have been introduced as movers and shakers of imbalance in an ad hoc social situation between two people, let's consider the chaos and upset civil society is experiencing today from their influence-creating imbalance in civil society at large. And further, let's go on to consider how this civil imbalance arises when the non-conceptual dimension of mind is not given its proper due.

The naturally spacious and timeless dimension of mind has very relevant characteristics:

I) Equanimity. The naturally timeless spaciousness of mind is equanimous. <u>Naturally equanimous</u>. That means it's <u>naturally</u> balanced, unlike the conceptual dimension of mind, which is discursive.

"Discursive" means it tends to run all over the place trying to make civil society equitable. That is, when it is motivated by tolerance and not pride and fear. Equality since The Declaration of Independence has been our guiding idea, as President Biden pointed out in his resignation speech, but we haven t given up on the idea as an ideal. Neither have we gone back to the days of overt state sanctioned intolerance (prejudice, bigotry, misogyny and slavery!). Unfortunately, because we are only trained to use the tools of the conceptual mind, we don't realize that those tools alone can't achieve the results they conceive and desire. The conceptual dimension of mind cannot by itself achieve civil equity because it is not itself equanimous. Straighten the chairs on the deck of the Titanic, if it pleases you, but that won't float the boat of an equanimous society. Such a society will not realize equality even if inequality is legislated out of existence. Even if outright bigotry and slavery are expunged, using forceful means to impose the legislation. That civil society is resting on a powder keg. An equanimous society only happens when the citizens enjoy the equanimity of mental balance. In addition, real readiness for this requires realistic preparation. I can be eagerly anticipating to run as a first timer in the Boston marathon, but if I am not really ready because of inadequate preparation, then I am "foolishing myself." Why? Because I am ignorant of not yet being "equal" to the challenge. We can plead for the fruits of a civil society; we can march for them; we can legislate for them; we can we can even try to enforce them. But until our minds are made equanimous, we won't ever enjoy the fruits of them. It has to be acknowledged, realized and inculcated into our pedagogy from the earliest get-go that imbalance simply breeds the bitter fruit of inequality.

Our educational system in the West (our pedagogy) is imbalanced. To the extent that it is, we are not ready to achieve a civil society that is tolerant, peaceful, respectful of the law, lovingly gracious to one another even more than being justly tolerant.

II) Equanimity once again. Another characteristic arising from an equanimous state of mind is fresh revelation. A mind open to fresh revelation does not fear change or innovation or novelty. The naturally spacious and timeless awareness dimension of mind has eliminated fear at its base and is well on its way to eliminating pride as a motivator. Consider how much unrest in civil society is based on, and arises out of, fear and pride. Trump's "Maganite" followers fear that their whitey-tightey dominance is ending, and it is. By 2050--no matter what the Maganites do--the white man will be in the minority in America. Trump's followers take unholy pride in their cult-like devotion to their golden-haired idol. The Evangelical Nationalists justify Trump's egregiously negative behavior by saying, "God writes straight with crooked lines." Trump may be a demonic thug, but that's who God has chosen to right the ship of state. Moreover, the Maganites both fear the loss of "their America," and again take unholy pride in believing it was given by god to people like them exclusively. And therefore, they are duty bound and devotionally motivated to throw out all the black and brown interlopers. First round 'em all up in detention camps; then fly them back to drop zones south of the border. Equanimity and an equanimous state of mind are totally absent in the Maganite agitators spoiling for a fight to "Make America Great Again." BTW: have you seen the Kamala Harris T-shirt? "M.A. L.A." in large letters: "Make America Laugh Again!"

It is much easier to see the lack of equanimity "out there" being exhibited by Maganites agitating for their version of society. It's much harder to acknowledge its absence in our own minds when we fight for the idea and ideals of Thomas Jefferson and our constitutional democracy. Nevertheless, the fact is that unrest and civil disturbance arise from mental unrest and mental disturbance. Mental balance requires mental equanimity and vice versa. Mental balance is impossible without becoming friendly and familiar with the naturally occurring timeless and spacious awareness dimension of our own mind. Straighten the

Titanic's deck chairs with geometric precision and equality according to your finest ideal conception, but that ship of state won't float, let alone make passage to the Port of Ideal Equality until our pedagogy acknowledges and trains us in the spacious equanimity of the non-conceptual dimension of mind.

Chapter Six: Conceptual Freshness

Our school teachers and professors don't require much memorization anymore. Oh, of course, there's plenty of cramming to momentarily memorize test stuff that will mostly be forgotten. Kids aren't required to memorize poems and important speeches. How, you ask, is such memorization connected to conceptual freshness? In the last chapter, I briefly discussed the manifestations in civil society of pride and fear. I touched upon the idea that an equanimous state of mind is a "place" where fresh revelation can occur: namely, novel ideas and innovations. Ok, but what has a memorized poem or speech got to do with that? A good question leading to a good answer (hopefully).

A memorized poem can be more comforting in times of stress than a hot tub or a dry martini. For example, I love Shakespeare's Sonnet 29. Graham Norton had Judi Dench on his show, along with Arnold Schwarzenegger and several others. Norton asked if Judi could recite something from memory, and she gave an impromptu recital of Sonnet 29:

When, in disgrace with fortune and men's eyes
I all alone beweep my outcast state
And trouble deaf heaven with my bootless cries
And look upon myself and curse my fate,

Wishing me like to one more rich in hope,
Featured like him, like him with friends possessed,
Desiring this man's art and that man's scope,
With what I most enjoy contented least;

Yet in these thoughts myself almost despising
Haply I think on thee, and then my state,
Like to the lark at break of day arising
From sullen earth, sings hymns at heaven's gate

For thy sweet love remembered such wealth brings
That then I scorn to change my state with kings.

Oh my, in times when one needs comfort and solace, a poem like this can put one back into that space of gracious equanimity and gratitude, despite the suffering that prompted one to think of it. However, if you were never asked to memorize it in school, you probably never did. Not even thinking about it, you reach in vain now for a comfort blanket and find only a pittance or a petulance in your pocket. Western pedagogy let you down.

Or who would not be moved to greater courage and fortitude by recalling the poem "If" by Rudyard Kipling? Let me quote just the first and last stanza, while urging the reader to read the entire poem.

If you can keep your head when all about you
    Are losing theirs and blaming it on you,
If you can trust yourself when all men doubt you
    But make allowance for their doubting too;
If you can wait and not be tired by waiting

Or being lied about, don't deal in lies,
Or being hated, don't give way to hating,
       And yet don't look too good, nor talk too wise:

If you can talk with crowds and keep your virtue,
       Or walk with Kings--nor lose the common touch.
If neither foes nor loving friends can hurt you,
       If all men count with you, but none too much;
If you can fill the unforgiving minute
       With sixty seconds' worth of distance run
Yours is the Earth and everything that's in it,
       And--what is more--you'll be a Man, my son!

I trust I don't need to belabor the application of Kipling's sentiments in this poem to the tumultuous times of civil unrest and personal distress we are now in. This poem, written in 1895 but not published until 1910 has been referenced many times and given people much inspiration. But how many could recite it from memory, on command or in dire need of its message without a cell phone to call it up? Graham Norton had Arnold Schwarzenegger and two others with him when he asked Judi Dench to recite something from Shakespeare from memory. Her rendition was beautiful, of course, but Arnold's comment was only slightly self-deprecating: "More text there than for me in most of my movies!" It struck me that in 2024, four educated adults should find it remarkable that someone could recite a sonnet from memory, in public no less. A sonnet is only 14 lines long, and a typical form is abba-abba-cde-cde. This is the so-called Petrarchan form that Milton used in his poem, "On His Blindness" or sometimes the first line is used as the title "When I consider how my light is spent," written sometime in mid-17th century, about fifty years after Shakespeare's Sonnet 29 written in 1592.

Milton is famous for his epic poems "Paradise Lost" and "Paradise Regained"--I don't know anyone who memorized either one of these epic poems. However, many Greek schoolboys in the 5th-3rd centuries BCE had memorized the 1500 lines of the <u>Iliad</u>, and the very best students would have also memorized the 12,109 lines of the <u>Odyssey</u> by the time they were graduating to higher education! Of course, Homer was their equivalent to our Bible. They studied Homer intensely, and since it was written in dactylic hexameter (long-short-short meter as in "This is dactylic the measure [meter] of Homer and Longfellow.") Not only did this meter chanted aloud lend itself to memorization, but it was studied out loud at school. There were no textbooks; parchment was scarce and expensive. Also, traveling bards would frequently visit town and entertain the folks with a dramatic Homeric recitation with lyre accompaniment. Homer would have been frequently quoted by people of the polis. Even so, think about having over 3000 lines of poetry memorized! Here is Milton's Sonnet 16, "On His Blindness":

> When I consider how my light is spent
> Ere half my days, in this dark world and wide,
> And that one Talent which is death to hide
> Lodged within me useless, though my soul more bent
> To serve therewith my Maker, and present

My true account, lest he returning chide,
"Doth God exact day-labour, light denied?"
I fondly ask. But patience to prevent
That murmur soon replies, "God doth not need
Either man's work or his own gifts, who best
Bear his mild yoke, they serve him best. His state
Is Kingly, thousands at his bidding speed,
And post o'er land and ocean without rest.
They also serve who only stand and wait.

This poem allows Milton to find acceptance and meaning in his blindness, a difficulty for anyone, let alone a poet. Still, he was able nevertheless to dictate his thoughts. But think of Beethoven losing his hearing and still able to compose memorable symphonies. Milton alludes, I think, to Matthew 25:15-40 in line 3 of the poem "And that one Talent which is death to hide."

In the Gospel parable, the landlord distributes talents to three stewards: 10-5, and 1 respectively. He expects a return on his "investment" upon his return. The stewards with 10 and 5 talents repay him handsomely by doubling their talents. But the third steward buried his talent and returns it without interest, saying he feared his hard-ass landlord, and it seemed better just to play it safe. The hapless steward gets his ass kicked out into the unforgiving darkness. And Mathew's parable ends with the puzzling (?) idea: to those who have been given much, even more will be given; but to those with little, even that will be taken away.

Milton may be associating himself with the hapless steward who didn't parlay or invest his talent so as to return it with interest. Perhaps it doesn't matter that "talent" In Matthew is probably coin money but in Milton it refers to poetic ability.

One of my favorite poems is from a Jesuit poet of the late 19th century, Gerard Manley Hopkins. This poem, also identified only by its first line, is typical of his innovative "sprung rhythm" and celebration of the divine manifesting in man and in all of creation. The poem "essentializes," if you will, a metaphysical tenet that the self is a substantial entity, stable and independent, manifesting God's glory when fully alive. This "realistic" philosophy so characteristic of western Christianity is typical of the philosophy I was inculcated with as a Jesuit scholastic. My three years in "the Philosophate" at Weston College west of Boston emphasized the metaphysics and epistemology derived mostly from Thomas Aquinas (1225-1274). Hopkins, however, favored the approach of John Duns Scotus (1266-1308). Poets tend to favor Scotus who celebrated the "particularities of things" as the essentially real; whereas Aquinas thought the universal essence of things gave them their reality. These opposing views have been debated in the West since Aristotle and Plato. The Buddha says, in effect, "I deny your major tenet, both of you." In my other books, I delve into the Buddhist philosophy that understands "emptiness" ("shunyata" in Sanskrit) as the essential reality. All phenomena are "empty" of essential self-nature which, correctly understood, allows for overcoming the illusion of our separation. Succinctly put, we are here to overcome the illusion of separation. Separation is suffering. Failing to see through the apparent reality of things' essentially separate selves creates the self-imposed prison of the Dualistic Matrix, which is the origin and context of all our suffering.

To return to this chapter's theme: memorized poetry (and the poet's composition of it) serves to give something like conceptual freshness or comforting salve when one feels blistered and buffeted by "the slings and arrows of outrageous fortune." Poetry provides profound consolation in times of distress. It refreshes; it opens the doorway to the naturally occurring timeless spacious awareness dimension of mind, that dimension which is naturally equanimous and a space of profound restfulness.

Here then is Hopkins' "As kingfishers catch fire" which celebrates a philosophic view of the self which-- Hopkins not realizing it--establishes a metaphysical separation between the human phenomenon and its Divine Source. Hopkins truly felt he was conceiving the opposite in his poetry. He is enamored of the divine manifesting in and through all created phenomena and human creativity. Nevertheless, the self as so conceived is unwittingly trapped in the Dualistic Matrix where separation reigns; appearances do not contradict this ultimate view of reality until and unless they are correctly understood in their emptiness, according to the Buddha.

> As kingfishers catch fire, dragonflies draw flame;
> As tumbled over rim in roundly wells
> Stones ring; like each tucked string tells, each hung bell's
> Bow swung finds tongue to fling out broad its name;
> Each mortal thing does one thing and the same:

Deals out that being indoors each one dwells;
Selves--goes itself; <u>myself</u> it speaks and spells
Crying <u>what I do is me</u>: for that I came.

I say more: the just man justices;
Keeps grace: that keeps all his goings graces;
Acts in God's eye what in God's eye he is--
Christ--for Christ plays in ten thousand places,
Lovely in limbs, and lovely in eyes not his
To the Father through the features of men's faces.

As I said, I love this poem. It makes me tear up. I can recite it with such feeling that people hearing it for the first time are stunned with its beauty. Kingfishers, it needs to be said by way of introduction perhaps, are birds highly active along English streams, bright blue and auburn in color, and iconic of Hopkins' vision of the dynamic beauty manifesting Divine glory in and through their own glorious being. For a long while, it's true, this poem essentialized my own philosophy and view of reality. So now, while I understand its metaphysical implications as inherently limiting (to me, anyway), I return to it often for the pleasure of the music, imagery and even friendship, like to one once close but then having drifted apart, we no longer share mutual karmic closeness.

The reason for reproducing some of my memorable (and memorized) poems is to illustrate my basic point: <u>pedagogy in the West is imbalanced</u>. Illustrative of this fact is that memorization of poetry and famous speeches (e.g., the Gettysburg Address) is not required anymore, when in my childhood and early teens it was commonplace. This memorization often included a recitation in front of the class. This practice familiarized students early on with public speaking and overcoming the fear of speaking in front of an audience. This is a skill that is patently lacking today. Civil public discourse is absent, let alone the ability to face a civil crowd with civility.

Recently the Surgeon General, Dr. Murthry, is recommending warnings (like on cigarette packs) of the dangers inherent in social media excess. It is estimated that kids today spend an average of 3-5 hours a day on Tik-tok et. al. This exposure (it appears there is increasing evidence) is leading to an increase of depression and anxiety that are being medically treated now. This rarely happened in my childhood. Kids are confronted with frequent body image critiques and impossible ideals. Not readily able to withstand these assaults, they become shy and/or defensive about how people perceive their bodies.

In closing, this chapter I want to mention a metallic black statue I recently saw called "The Weight of Thought" (by Belgian sculptor, Thomas Lerooy). This large sculpture shows a man sitting on a ledge, his body is skeletally lean, but his head is hugely disproportional to the rest of his body. He is effortly supporting it in his hands as the weight makes him lean far down and forward. "The Weight of Thought" is not a portrait of mental balance. This poor guy has no balance from the spacious, restful dimension of the naturally clear, limitless dimension of his non-conceptual mind. This is a picture of conceptual overload! This is definitely not a portrait of conceptual freshness or poetic refreshment. The sculptor has captured a painful embodiment of how the discursive, conceptual, busy and label-filled dimension of mind can be so overloaded as to weigh heavy with almost debilitating thought--debilitating, that is, when not <u>balanced</u> by the naturally occurring timeless and spacious awareness dimension of mind.

> "If this be error and upon me proved/ I never writ, nor no man ever loved. (Shakespeare, Sonnet 116)

Chapter Seven: Delightfully Nosey

My seven-year-old granddaughter "Z" (short for Zanna, short for Suzanna) showed up suddenly with her dad and three big (!) older brothers. They were coming home from a two-week beach vacation. My wife and I hadn't had a visit from Z in quite some time. She is actively alert, so curious and perceptive. She notices immediately anything that's different from her last visit three months ago! She goes about the house picking up "treasures" for taking with her back to her house. This visit my wife allowed her to take home the little blue stuffed dog that was given to us at the birth of her oldest brother, Leo, 16 years ago. Zanna also rummaged through drawers beneath our captains bed. On Carol's side Z found mostly winter clothes; she also found a long blue silk scarf that reminds me of one of my favorite song lyrics, a line from Al Stewart's "The Year of the Cat": "She comes out of the sun in a silk dress running like a water color in the rain." Wow! Shakespeare hasn't written a more beautiful line! Well, Z "coveted" this scarf, so Care Bear graciously gave it to her. There is also her special cup, tucked away inside the sideboard that Z always wants a drink from. It has a little bear sitting inside. It's her special cup at grandma's, and she allows that it should stay here for when she requests Care Bear's special sparkling water or hot chocolate, depending on the season.

It must be admitted, my granddaughter is delightfully nosey. But are we? And why or why not? What would being "delightfully nosey" look like in an adult, you might be asking yourself? And further, what's it got to do with mental imbalance leading to civil unrest? Very good. Better questions lead to better answers.

There's an expression I haven't heard used in a while: "It was like she had a veil over her eyes." And the comment is not a compliment about a lace-wedding veil or some other kind slipping down over her face unintended. No, a comment like this refers to something clouding clear vision. What is it, the comment actually wonders, that creates a kind of mental fog between the viewer's eyes and the object viewed, be it physical, metaphysical or completely conceptual?

In the Buddhist spiritual technology toolkit, one can find this paradoxical conceptual tool: <u>Impermanence as the Key to Wisdom</u>. I underline this phrase because it is actually the subtitle to my book, <u>Don't Foolish Yourself</u>. That book is an homage to my late root teacher, the Ven. Gyaltrul Rinpoche, referencing the Buddhist philosopher, Nagarjuna (c. 150-250CE); both teachers emphasize impermanence as the key to the wisdom of enlightenment.

Gyaltrul Rinpoche, following Nagarjuna, would often say something like, "You can't meditate too deeply or long enough on impermanence. Impermanence is key; it's your ticket to ride." Nagarjuna called impermanence the "backdoor" to the "house" of shunyata (i.e., emptiness of self as essentially independent).

A friend of mine recently lost his beloved wife of twenty years to cancer quite suddenly. He regards himself as a Buddhist. He even drove a long way to spend a weekend as part of a month long retreat being given at a Buddhist retreat center in upstate New York. But he left retreat early Sunday morning because the teachings being given as this retreat began were about impermanence, and he "wasn't getting much out of it." He felt he knew all he needed to know about impermanence because of dealing with the death of his wife. Big Mistake.

When asked to consider impermanence, people easily acknowledge certain changes happening: the seasons, fashions, innovations. Those more scientifically inclined mention atomic and subatomic activity where what can be observed appears to "blink on and off." Then there's the macrocosmic swirl and dance of galaxies that the Huble and James Webb telescopes have given us stunning and romantic images of.

Curiously, however, when at my imagined kiosk at the mall where Peanuts' character Lucy is attending, and she asks passersby this question: "Do you think that people change?" What is the answer most people give, do you think? Well, I think most people say, "Of course in some ways some change is obvious. We all age. That's a big change. We have kids and start families. Another big change. Sometimes we even change our diets or appetites, and ask for broccoli or brussel sprouts from the restaurant menu! But character change...well, not so much. Actually, where character is concerned, people don't change." Now granted, that passerby was unusually verbal. Most people, "Yeah, maybe in some ways, but not in others."

Now, without the possibility of radical character change, the Buddha's entire game plan is a ridiculous farce, and worse, a criminal deceit foisted on a gullible public. What is the <u>only</u> thing, according to the Buddha, that goes with you through the portal of death? According to Christian scripture, not even a sesame seed. And Islam has a saying, I think, that says "a shroud has no pockets." Same idea. According to the Buddha all you take through the portal of death is the gestalt of your habitual tendencies. Shorthand: your character. Frankly, if there is no character change--even possible--you're screwed. Imagine taking everlasting rebirths with a never-changing character riddled with faults and malfeasance. Imagine that there is no default or fallback rebirth posture to save your sorry self from what? From another rebirth that is even worse than the suffering of the last one! If character change is not possible (practically doable and already modeled by beings like us who have achieved the character change that frees them from negative self-serving habits), then we're all still screwed.

You know change can be scary, or it can even be just funny. On a podcast recently, I watched small children suddenly and unexpectedly be surprised by their dad having shaved off his beard. These little ones either cried, ran away or usually both. They had to be coaxed to be comforted and reassured; mostly by their dad's voice <u>and</u> smell that eased their transition. From my viewer's distance, the experience of children being startled and scared by this change was belly-laugh funny.

Funny in a very different way was a recent experience involving my forty-two year old son who had just come to visit on his way home from a two-week beach vacation with his four kids. My wife and I had just that morning groomed the front yard to practically immaculately conceived conditions: grass cut just so, trimming done around the night-lights, nary a weed in sight. And to boot, the previous week we had all the trees in the front yard professionally trimmed. Nevertheless, Jeff (whose from yard is postage stamp in size with narly roots like varicose veins showing above ground around the one untrimmed maple tree) gets out of the car and delivers a micro managed critique that the blue spruce ground cover at the edge of the road needs more color! Where did this suddenly acute nurseryman's comment spring from? My wife and I laughed heartedly about it later, actually thrilled that our older son was not only taking an interest in the look of our yard but was offering to help! Now that's FUNNY...in a droll sort of way.

Here's the point relative to the profound and pervasive phenomenon of universal impermanence: <u>what changes when we notice what went unnoticed before</u>? Here's the profound philosophic point: We habitually and conceptually impose "the same" (as in "the <u>same</u> river") on what is changing every nano second. Why, you ask, should I care? The question: why should I care about minute --even imperceptible--changes in my environment when I can make perfectly good sense (mundane and common) to almost everyone? Superlatively good questions provoke superlatively (even life changing) answers: <u>Because your future rebirth depends upon it</u>. Have I got your attention?

"Wait, wait...hold on there, professor. My future rebirth is conditioned in some way by my perception or misperception of small (even minute) change(s)? Is that what I hear you telling me? Oh boy, this'll be good!"

When the Buddha says: all suffering originates from a perceptual mistake, he first identifies that mistake with taking the self to be real <u>in a way it is not</u>. Secondly, we go on to extrapolate that mistake by taking all other phenomena to be real <u>in a way they are not</u>. To be real in a mistaken way: that means we mistake appearances to be something they're not. What not? The "same"! This matters in each and every personal encounter by which our character develops as we behave (thoughts, words and deeds) according to misperceptions that blithely go unrecognized.

In many of my other books, I detail this mistake as it takes place on the most obvious (?) and grossest level. That is, "the other" we perceive as separate in a way that creates the subject-object polarity of the dualistic matrix (the confining context of our own self-imprisonment in the never-ending cyclic existence of suffering). We further go on to conceptualize "the other" as potentially <u>object</u>ionable. That is, sooner or later that other will stand in my way in some way or other. Whether it's by blaming or "neutralizing" the other, we do what we must to eliminate this object as obstacle. From this nuclear source arises all negativity: confrontational aggression, hostile competition, violence, belligerence and war. "Take it down a notch, professor, if you would, please." Ok.

Those neighbors down the street, "the same ones" you always a) sidestep or ignore b) make small talk with c) avoid talking politics or religion with d) sometimes maybe energetically debate both: one of those folks is now at your door; and you spoke last to him/her about two weeks ago. If they are perceived as "just the same," you've imposed a conceptual label that releases you from any close attention to this person or their visit. The result, "same ole, same ole."

The universe is abundantly present in its ceaseless outpouring of changing, impermanent phenomena, and we can't be bothered to notice. The gracious prodigality of the universe pours forth its abundance without a "hook"; that is, it takes no umbrage if it doesn't get a thank-you card or even an acknowledgement from us in return. But the universe tends to scowl darkly with attentiveness when we don't share our abundance. "What abundance?" you ask. "Have you seen the way I live?" You have the ability to be <u>abundantly</u> <u>attentive</u>. That means making the effort to notice what would otherwise pass imperceptibly in your neighbor at your door. According to a calculus applied by the universe, perhaps the greatest gift you have to offer is your completely undivided attention. Reflect: what is that veil that fogs or obscures the clarity of our vision? It's our habits, our habitual propensity to be mentally and emotionally lazy. The "same ole, same ole" is easy. Taking account of and making the minimally perceptible count, that's hard. Why? Because of the habitual mental tendencies to impose lazy old categories on what is ever fresh and new, if we are awake to it. Sleep walking mechanicality will get you a repetitive rebirth in all probability worse than the one you've been given this time around. If you don't believe me or the Buddha, check in with what Jesus has to say in Matthew 25: 15-40. The overlord gave various talents to three stewards. Check out what happened to the one who didn't parlay his to his own or his overlord's benefit.

The present, as has been said, is the perpetual gift of the universe. Take it for granted at your peril. This chapter builds on the last called "Conceptual Freshness." The secret of youth is youthfulness. No, not a tautology. Nature obliges kids to face novelty every day. They usually eat it up. Old farts are stale because they allowed the oasis of new beginnings to dry up. Finding yourself imprisoned horribly, your ultimate freedom is your ability to adopt an attitude about your present and future. Imprisoned in the mindset that always takes the day's appearances to be just what they seem is a self-made prison. And the securest prison is the one you don't even know you're in.

If, as Gyaltrul Rinpoche advised, impermanence is your "ticket to ride," one had best get off the speeding train to "the next best thing" which quickly becomes "that old thing." Start by turning over the mental stone of "same ole something or someone" and discover the universe's gift of the ever new present.

Have I managed to wander away from the chapter title's theme: being delightfully nosey? Well, it may seem that adult attention to the impermanence of details is a long way from a child's delightfully nosey search for treasures at grandma's. It's not. In the next chapter I'll try to connect the dots so that the virtually imperceptible becomes, if not delightfully, then painfully obvious.

Chapter Eight: Readiness for Personal Revelation

Back when I was a grad student in philosophy at Fordham University in NYC, I would often take a break by walking in the nearby Bronx Botanical Gardens. One memorable day stands out. I was reading Walt Whitman's <u>Leaves of Grass</u>. The line "all flesh is grass" leapt out at me. Usually, this thought is interpreted as a "memento mori"; that is, it's a reminder of one's mortality. Like the grass of the fields that brown out, wither and die, so do we all; all flesh is like that grass in the field. On this day, however, my mind turned that phrase upside down, as it were to: <u>all grass is flesh</u>. The meaning to me was crystal clear, studying, as I was to become a priest in the Society of Jesus. As a priest, one's ordination in the Catholic Church is universally regarded as an empowerment that enables the words of the priest at Mass ("This is my body. This is my blood.") of consecration to substantially change the bread and wine into Christ's body and blood. Allowing for the appearances to remain the same, the essence or substantial reality is believed to be changed into the actual body (flesh) and blood of Jesus the Christ. My personal revelation that day awakened me to: ALL GRASS IS FLESH; to me that means that Divine nurture can be contacted, "tasted and consumed" anywhere. That is, "all grass" equates to all phenomena. Divinity is manifest and embodied everywhere. The only thing obstructing that realization is that veil of unawareness. If one finds Divine food everywhere and experiences being fed and nurtured by it, who's to say "No." Let that pedant of a sophist try to argue me into being hungry after that ten course meal; the fact is that I am feeling completely fed, full and satisfied. If I am then I am. If the Divine can feed us anywhere, who's to say "No"? In other words (Big Moment for this priest-to-be), Eucharist, in effect, can be taken not just at the communion rail during Mass, but you can take it anywhere if your awakened awareness makes it so! Is the Church really in a position to say, "No, now really let me tell you why you're still hungry?!

It may not be obvious how the last three chapters ("Imbalance and the Mind of Civility," "Conceptual Freshness," and "Delightfully Nosey") exemplify or develop this book's title: <u>Readiness Is All</u>. Well, in Chapter Five, our "readiness to blame" came up for discussion, and also perhaps our ingenuous readiness to say "I'm sorry" as maybe just being the equivalent of a throat clearing. In Chapter Six we discussed how our pedagogical imbalance, exemplified by not having our kids memorize poetry or important speeches anymore perhaps, leaves us less than ready and prepared for moments of stress and times of distress. Having the powerfully comforting thoughts of writers who deeply experienced suffering and were able to put into words ("what oft was thought yet ne'er so well expressed") what for most of us is ineffable, we miss out on that kind of readiness, in my opinion. Wouldn't it be better if we could be ready to address our suffering with something immediately "at hand" because memorized? Why do we miss out on that?

Chapter Seven touched upon a rather subtle epistemological idea: namely, we put a conceptual "veil" between the perceptions of phenomena that are constantly changing with our static interpretations. Failing to give our full, undivided attention to what the universe is "presenting" us with moment by moment, we develop the hard as horn habits of lazy disregard and a readiness to misperceive what is really fresh and new. Our habit is to perceive and say "same ole, same ole."

The experience I had in the Bronx Botanical Gardens I treasure as a moment of revelation to me personally. I regard it as a moment of revelation to me personally as a gift from All That Is divinely manifesting in all that is. In my opinion, what made it possible was a readiness and openness for greater soul depth in search of greater spiritual depth. Scripture says that doors open if one continues to knock. That's a metaphorical way of saying, "Answers come only to questions." A contrary metaphor says, "If the only tool you've got is a hammer, everything looks like a nail." Translated: if your readiness is so narrowly focused that only one thing seems suitable, it's likely much will be missed or even great harm done. For example, imagine a grease fire on the stove and you've been told to only use baking soda not water. Searching in vain for baking soda, the fire starts to burn the overhead microwave. Alternate solution: just cover the fire with the lid of the cast iron pot that's on another burner. In other words, smother the fire with something else. Baking soda is not your only option! Narrow focus, narrow results...or none.

In the Buddhist tradition, there is an extraordinary methodology of mindfulness. It is totally nonsectarian and non-confrontational. It is compatible with prayer practices from any faith-based tradition. What it does, from the point of view of this book, is to make the mind <u>ready</u> for personal revelation. It is sometimes said that the spiritual technology of the Buddha is basically technology for garbage clean up. According to the Buddha, the mind is pristinely characterized as a dimension of naturally occurring timeless and spacious awareness. This dimension mostly goes unnoticed because of the mental clutter and conceptual "garbage" that's in the way. A frequent TV ad for a company called "Got Junk?" shows delighted homemakers snapping their fingers at ugly, cluttered garages, and suddenly the Got Junk folks have cleaned up and cleared out that garbage. Amazingly, the garbage has been restored to its original pristine spaciousness!

<u>If</u> the motivating question--like the one that moved me out of the limited fruitfulness and nurture of the Society of Jesus--is how to develop greater soul depth for the sake of greater spiritual depth, <u>then</u> the questioner has to be <u>ready</u> for some serious garbage clean-up. Readiness is all-important because all the garbage must go. In fact, all the major esoteric spiritual traditions that I am familiar with state: "When the student is ready, the teacher will appear." I mean absolutely no disrespect when I say that a really good teacher is a "garbage guru." Please don't mistake my meaning. The guru knows how to help the student

identify the garbage, especially the mental and emotional clutter that momentarily hides from view (there's that veil again). And what does it hide from view? The naturally occurring timeless and spacious dimension of the students' own awareness.

In the book, I wrote titled, <u>You Make Me So Fat: Why Be Bothered by Blaming</u>, I challenge the reader to accept responsibility for all their own feelings. So, why does the syntactically similar statement, "You make me so mad I could..." sound not only plausible but reasonable? Yet upon closer examination, it is revealed how it is another one of those egregious misperceptions that mistake the appearances for reality.

The motivating rationale behind blaming is similar to the ones that declare, "It's so unfair" and "Woe is me, I'm such a victim of (you name it)." "Blame," unfair" and "victim" can be used as the wallet-sized summary of basic Buddhist practice, much like the wallet-sized AARP card summarizes one's benefits for their $16.00 yearly subscription.

"Ok, professor," you protest. "That may be so. I haven't read your other book. But please explain how these "no-no's" relate to the overall theme of "Readiness is all." Be glad to. Blaming, claiming to be unfairly treated and victimized are examples of mental garage garbage clutter. Until these mental habits that clutter the mind are thoroughly cleared, there is no readiness to go for greater soul depth in search of greater spiritual depth.

My Botanical Garden revelation didn't instantly become an habitual perception. "One swallow doesn't make a summer," as they say about Capistrano. How long does it take to solidify a habit? Now that's a really good "rock candy ponderable." A lot could be learned from the patient study of one's own habits and their development over time. A) How did they arise? B) What impediments were there to practicing them? (Being careful to note the differences between developing good vs. bad habits) C) What efforts did it take to change a habit, for example, smoking, drinking to excess, gossiping, etc? D) How long did it take to change a bad habit or solidify a good one? E) Which habits count as garbage clutter? F) Why the resistance to clear out the garbage clutter? Personally speaking, I have been trying to stay awake to the revelation "All grass is flesh" (i.e., divine nurture) for almost fifty years, and I still go hungry from missing an obvious meal.

It seems to me that good habits are an ongoing process to incorporate those benefits ever more completely. "Perfection" is not the goal. In fact, as I try to point out in my book, <u>Complete, Not Completed</u> (found within <u>Applied Spirituality, Intermediate Level</u>, Vol 2.1), "perfection" is a subtle and invidious trap we've been unwittingly told to adopt from the Greeks. Today (7-30-24) I watched Simone Biles lead the US women's Olympic gymnastics team to a gold medal in Paris. Simone is 27 years old; that's old for a gymnast. She is the greatest gymnast of all time, yet she is still developing her skills. She competes with stellar grace, beauty and performance excellence, yet her gold medal represents but another plateau, a completion open to further moments of completion.

"Moments of completion"--that is what the universe is presenting us with at every moment. Sadly, we misperceive, misinterpret or just can't be bothered to notice. When the impermanence of things slams us to the mat with a jolt of unexpected suffering, perhaps someone, kindly intent on salving our hurt, might say, "And this too shall pass." Everything passes; everything is impermanent. Healing and wholeness result not from believing "better times are just ahead"--the implication of "this too shall pass." Healing and wholeness welcome change and partner with it to achieve momentary plateaus (some high, some low) of completion.

In the next chapter, the theme is mental garbage clean up as it relates to our cosmic future.

Chapter Nine: Mental Garbage Clean-up

In the last chapter, I raised about six questions as I broached the topic of cosmic garbage clean up and how our mental habits necessitate it. For some time I have been dealing with an aggravating pain in my right thigh that feels like a muscle cramp, but treating it like a muscle cramp does not relieve the pain. Recently I was in hospital rehab recovering from a stroke that turned my right leg into a wet noodle. Currently I can walk haltingly with a walker, but that thigh pain remains unchanged and undiagnosed, though the rehab doctors examined it with a battery of tests. Currently, my outpatient rehab PT assistants are intrigued. They regard me as an enigma wrapped in a conundrum, but hey, I give them a curious change in their normal rehab routines. Yesterday I had a "PET" scan, which I do every six months to keep track of my renal cell carcinoma--so actually I'm really very healthy except for being a cripple with cancer!

Perhaps the reader has come across the phrase, "What resists, persists." Catchy. The wholesome and healing idea behind that pithy expression is this: what one puts resistance up against is paradoxically energized by that resistance. It tends, therefore, to resist change more energetically for the better than it otherwise would _if_. _If_ what? Paradoxically, if the problem (pain, for example) were "relaxed" into. For example, newbie meditators often make the mistake of energetically trying to resist the onset of their disquieting thoughts by applying mental forcefulness, like an invisible tourniquet, to stop their thoughts. This effort to forcefully resist actually energizes the thoughts. They persist and become even more bothersome and distracting. The mindfulness methodology of the Buddha has many tool kit techniques that apply here, but one is to relax, let go and just notice those thoughts. They will arise willy-nilly because they are habitual. It's natural; you can't force them not to. However, just like noticing the passing clouds overhead, if not energized by your engagement, letting your resistance relax, that is, they (the thoughts) will naturally and of their own accord slowly quiet down and diminish.

In the PET scan tube my thigh pain--lying flat aggravates it--prompted fruitless resistance. So, what I did instead was to "breathe deeply into" the pain. Rather than resistance by some sort of self-distraction, I put my full and complete attention on that thigh pain and "managed" it with my breath. The pain relaxed and became more tolerable and the time passed more quickly. Try remembering: "What resists, persists"--explore and test the results for yourself, like any good empirical science would do.

So the question to focus on for Chapter Nine is: which habits of mind count as "garbage clutter"? In other words, 1) given the all-pervasive phenomena of impermanence (everything in the universe is constantly changing) and 2) how does this impermanence contribute (pros vs. cons) to Readiness Is All? And to get quite specific 3) is this impermanence (the constantly changing phenomena of the universe) a help or a hindrance to that naturally occurring timeless and spacious awareness of mind?

Ok, then. Open wide that "garage door" so that you--and only you can see it and do it--take an account and complete a tabulation of the clutter that you find there. And direct the focus of your investigation to the habit(s) of mind that perpetuate and compound the clutter. While allowing time for that "rock candy ponderable" to dissolve deeply into your mind, let me tell an illustrative story.

I once lived in a town house adjacent to a very nice couple. I'll call the fellow, Martin, to protect his anonymity. Martin openly acknowledged his OCD condition. Once my wife and I went away and left our dog in Martin's care. As a "thank you" for his kind attention to our pup, we bought Martin a small gift: a white ceramic finger-bowl sized dish with an animal--I forget which, a raccoon, maybe-- on the lid and the raccoon's family nesting inside. Well, Martin's attraction to this figurine gave birth to about 75 purchases of similar figurines within a six-month period. He had to buy a display cabinet to house them all! Martin's wife told us, "Don't you ever bring him a gift like that again!" Now collecting figurines might be a benign, albeit expensive, habit. And if uncontrollable, might clutter the house. But the mind?

Let's return to the habitual mental clutter, especially those habits of mind that veil the naturally occurring timeless and spacious awareness dimension. Test yourself against this scenario: You let yourself in through a neighbor's front door, walk through the living room and on through the dining room to the kitchen on the way to the back deck barbecue that your and the neighbors have been invited to. Question: How many judgments did you make (positive and negative) about the interior of the house in the time, it took you to get to the deck? Don't know how many? How many items in your own attic or garage that your wife is eager to discard? Don't know even though it's been how many times for how long that she's been bugging you about it? That's mental clutter going unnoticed. Things that after some time in meditation practice you begin to notice (especially the judgments!).

Back a judgment up and what do you find? 1) perceptual phenomena 2) conceptualization of those perceptions "organized" into 3) interpretations of basically <u>like</u> and <u>dislike</u> and finally 4) judgments which generally solidify your pre-existing habits reflecting, in your case, your fashion and furniture preferences. All this passes virtually unnoticed. It's mental clutter, and if it was simply innocuous stuff accumulated over time, but is now unused (like attic and garage "junk"). Perhaps harmless enough. But judgments unfortunately are not merely harmless mental clutter. Instinctive judgments arising out of unexamined habits are prejudicial veils hiding, disguising or discarding (due to mental habits of attraction and aversion) what the universe is momentarily offering you as the gift of the present.

Habitual judgments made on the basis of unexamined biases of attraction and aversion are an affront to the patient prodigality (that is, its selfless generosity) of the universe. They basically say, "I can't be bothered to be freshly attentive to what's novel and new about this moment. Same ole, same ole is good enough for me." Unexamined habitual judgments reflect a <u>diminished readiness </u>to be alive to the fresh, youthful and momentary ad hoc completion being offered by the universe. Such instinctive, unreflective habits of mind are perhaps what Socrates had in mind when Plato had him say, "The unexamined life is not worth living."

The universe tolerates men mental garbage but finds it an unattractive and unreceptive place to deliver fresh and refreshing personal revelations. All That Is, by virtue of its unceasing and pristine timeless and spacious clarity, is more than ready to share its abundant yet momentarily hidden treasures. Anyone whose complementary naturally occurring timeless and spacious clarity of awareness shows itself ready is a suitable vessel. Unveiled is vessel-ready. Readiness is all it takes to find All That Is manifesting its Divinity in and through all that is. Once the mental clutter is cleaned up completely, Readiness Is All there is.

In the next chapter we tackle the difficult subject (and often intractable impediment) of how to turn frustration on its head and find it funny, if not always fun.

Chapter Ten: Frustration Can Be Funny

Frustration is not high up on the list of things people engage for fun. We dislike it. At least I'm not a fan. It usually comes as a distasteful and undesirable surprise. Frustration arises when our hard, honest, persevering efforts come either to nothing, not much or an unexpected disappointment.

Two friends of mine are beloved married partners. Best friends to each other and lovers who have endured the more and less of marriage for several decades. Unfortunately, one partner (call him Allen) is suffering from dementia; he exhibits behavior that his partner (call him Ben) finds very challenging to adjust to. Frankly, Ben finds lots of Allen's behavior very frustrating. Allen finally acknowledged his cognitive decline; and using an analogous pattern to Elizabeth Kubler-Ross' "five stages of grief," Allen is in stage #5, acceptance. Ben himself has had to learn patient virtues through his own stages of adjustment. In the early stages, his frustration would erupt because he felt that Allen was not making enough effort to address and compensate for his mental mishaps. These often "caused" Ben frustration, the kind Italian slang calls "agita." Agita is a blend of acidic irritation, agitation and frustration that can range from one to whatever on the Scoville hot pepper scale. Ben found it frustrating to talk to Allen about these matters because Allen was not inclined to talk about these matters. They gave <u>him</u> agita.

What helped Ben adjust and regain new equilibrium in the midst of very unsettling circumstances? Shameless self-promotion here: Ben read Robert Colacurcio's book, <u>You Make Me So Fat: Why Be Bothered by Blaming</u>. It took some mental and emotional recalibration, but Ben came to first understand that he <u>himself</u> had to take ownership and responsibility for feeling frustrated. Allen wasn't "making" Ben frustrated. The causality for Ben's feeling frustrated wasn't coming from "out there" in Allen. Ben had to acknowledge and deeply accept that his feelings were his own personal responsibility. He was simply wrong to blame Allen for his feelings of frustration. The statement (A) "You make me so frustrated" is not a causal equivalent to (B) "The rain makes me so sleepy." Although the two sentences are syntactically the same, the causality is entirely different. Rain causing sleepiness has empirically confirmed physical components having to do with the amount of oxygen in the atmosphere and the amount of sunlight. Frustration only appears to have an "out there" causal agency. We normally--until better tutored and less ignorant--take the statement, "He makes me so agita I could..." as plausible and probably even reasonable if we could know the facts. No, in fact it's not correct to blame anyone or anything "out there" for what I'm feeling. In fact--and this makes many people do a 180 degree about face from Buddhism--we must take responsibility for every experience we have. This means not just the negative, painful and frustrating experiences, but each and all the beneficent, rewarding and joyful ones too. This book is not the place to develop the cogent and conclusive argument why this is true. Try one of my other books on for size; what merit they may have, they are at least all small in size. But the emotions that arise upon our being in any given situation do not have the situation "out there" as cause, appearances to the contrary notwithstanding. Just as it's clear that the statement, "You make me so fat I could..." is fatuous foolishness; even so, "You make me so mad (frustrated, agita or whatever) is a mistake in the entire judgmental process: a) perceptual phenomena leading to b) conceptualizing and labeling c) crystalized with a false interpretation and d) solidified with incorrect and mistaken judgments.

Ben is a compassionate partner and desperately wants to "be there for" his partner. In other words, his intentions to be helpful were totally sincere, yet by themselves insufficient in their results. I'm reminded of the Peanuts cartoon. Charles Shulz has Charlie Brown downcast on the pitcher's mound having just served up another homerun ball. Charlie mutters, "Why am I such a failure? I'm so sincere!" Sincerity wasn't enough to increase Charlie Brown's delivery, speed or accuracy. His "meatball" pitches over the center of the plate "made" batters fat. That is, they got lots of hits to increase their batting averages. However, besides sincerity, Ben had something else going for him. He had developed friendly familiarity with the naturally occurring timeless spacious awareness dimension of his own mind. Resting there one day--like me resting in the Bronx Botanical Gardens with Walt Whitman--this "revelation" came to him. Most of Allen's bizarre behavior could be conceived to be just comical. If this behavior was deliberately cast by a director of SNL for a late night skit, there would be lots of humor in it. Now let's be clear: Ben is not reinterpreting Allen's forgetfulness as something "to make fun of." He's not laughing at Allen in the aspect of schadenfreude." Schadenfreude is a word English has adopted from German. Literally it means "joy in one's shade." That is, taking unholy joy in another's misfortune, failure or mishaps. Ben is not doing schadenfreude.

Frustration has a comical side. One condition of seeing otherwise frustrating events that way is the ability to laugh at oneself. Former President Donald Trump has never laughed at himself. He is, however, a prime exemplar of the practice of schadenfreude. It comes easily to him because it is characteristic of all bullies. To be able to see how one's own behavior--irritating to both oneself and another perhaps--can be interpreted as comical is an indication of mental spaciousness. People unable to laugh at themselves are way too serious, reflecting a mind with little spacious quiet, clarity and light-heartedness. As the saying goes, "The angels can fly because they take themselves lightly."

Ben quite suddenly and unexpectedly realized that he could "see" Allen's distracted wandering in search of his glasses perched on his forehead or his phone that he couldn't find in the dark, cave like recesses of his shoulder purse--now that's funny!

How does this simple yet profound moment of personal revelation relate to our themes: readiness is all. Ben had <u>made</u> <u>himself</u> <u>ready</u> because of a practice he'd been remembering from the spiritual technology tool kit of the Buddha. According to the Buddha, we need to be constantly observing our conceptions, interpretations and judgments. We allow mental clutter to accumulate when we don't. Recall the fellow passing from his neighbor's front door through the living room, dining room and kitchen. How many habitual judgments did he make in that short span of time? All this mental activity went completely unnoticed and unaccounted for. The Buddha's mindfulness methodology puts one on notice to pay close attention to the mind's habitual accumulations. This mindfulness practice adds a very challenging addendum: those people who frustrate irritate and "make" you "agita"--they are in fact <u>your teachers in disguise</u>.

The Buddha's spiritual technology is thoroughly empirical. Every hypothesis proposed to the student as a way to theoretically conceive and interpret some phenomena of experience is developed experientially until personal, empirical evidence gives the student confidence in a verified answer. Such answers are not based on faith or trust in authority. Personal experience, not belief, is the key and the test. The Buddha says: it may not initially appear to you this way, but those who irritate you the most are your best spiritual teachers. In disguise. Of course, <u>they</u> don't realize their function as teachers. Probably just the opposite. But then, isn't it the case that illusion is rampant throughout all phenomena? Everyone all the time is mistaking the self to be real in a way it is not, and consequently all other phenomena (irritating situations from the sides of <u>both</u> subject and object) are mistakenly perceived, conceived, interpreted and habitually judged to be <u>so</u> in ways that <u>are not so</u>.

How ready are you right now to step into a grad student chem lab, know how to find (let alone operate) an electron microscope, and then interpret correctly what you might (or might not) see when looking through it? My point? Readiness requires preparation. Often a lot of preparation. A lot of technical training and facility must precede correct use of such lab equipment. Maybe even more training and preparation when dealing with "mental equipment." So, for example, without hours spent observing both the movements of the conceptual dimension of mind plus hours spent observing the quiet stillness of the awareness (i.e., the non-conceptual) dimension of mind, there is probably minimal readiness to perceiving "that irritating asshole" as my teacher in disguise.

Similarly, the revelation that frustration can be funny, plus remembering to practice this insight in opposition to one's habitual tendency to become frustrated--that takes lots of prep to be ready.

Like the exercise of free will, readiness runs a spectrum of actual behaviors in practice. In other books, I delved into the nature of free will. It's my experience that readiness to grasp its actual behavior in practice takes lots of prep to be ready. Regarding free will, to be ready for what? To be ready to grasp that (a) while free will may be a given at birth as an integral component of the spirit-in-matter composite human being, (b) the actual exercise of free will flows like a river along a spectrum between the two camps on either side of the river. Camp #1: "Yes, there is." Camp #2: "No, there isn't." That is, some behaviors that appear to be the result of free will are actually habitual mechanical behaviors posing or disguised as free will. In other words, the actual behavior or exercise of free will is not an all or nothing thing. Some a little more, some a little less. Readiness is like that.

What it takes to get ready for your first dance is different from what it takes to graduate with honors from your high school STEM curriculum. So, here's another of those "rock candy ponderables": Is there any human behavior that didn't require some degree of readiness preparation in order to execute it? And I'm not considering a sudden assault that knocks you half-conscious from the back of a truck or some such. Rather, any behavior that has the <u>appearance</u> at least of free will involved--are there any that didn't require some kind of readiness preparation? If not, that might be another meaning to take from "Readiness is All."

Chapter Eleven: Planted Squarely in Mid-Air

A Google search quickly identifies the expression "Readiness is all" as from Shakespeare's <u>Hamlet</u>, Act 5, Scene 2. Defying the indications of augury (a method of divinization or fortune telling) it's a little ironic coming from the mouth of Hamlet to his friend Horatio. Hamlet is practically known as "Mr. Waffle," that is he's not known for his decisiveness. The most famous speech, perhaps, in all of English literature is his "To be or not to be" soliloquy where he reveals his waffle-headedness. But at this stage of the play, Hamlet has the four corners of his mind, if not anchored in stone, surely planted squarely in mid-air.

"Planted squarely in mid-air" is not meant as sarcasm. In the Vajrayana tradition of Tibetan Buddhism that I practice, we sometimes like to picture it as an ideal posture. The bogus solidity of apparent reality has revealed its deceptive substantiality. "Both feet planted squarely in mid-air" acknowledges one's awareness of the mirage-like quality of appearances. Their dream-like nature is not the firm ground we appear to stand on. Maybe, in fact, it's the best place from which to take a firm stand against "the slings and arrows of outrageous fortune." Mid-air readiness is a wiser, more acute observational posture from which to get a clear view <u>on</u> and a clear escape <u>from</u> the deceptiveness of appearances.

In my view, having had both of my feet planted squarely in mid-air for some time now, "Readiness is All" ought to be adopted as a guiding corrective to the imbalance of our western educational system. Our western pedagogy currently primes our students only for readiness of a certain kind. It (A) trains and habituates them to be forward looking: what's "the next best thing?" At one time, not so very long ago, cultured adults were persuaded that the past had something important to tell them, some iconic models of wisdom, statesmanship, honor and fidelity as well as examples of human performance excellence. It was taken for granted that it was surely practical to keep them in mind. At the very least, such mindfulness offered not a little protection against thoughtlessness that encouraged vulnerability. No more. About 400-500 years ago, a sea change happened. Since then we no longer look to the past to "mine golden mindfulness." The future is where it's at for today's tomorrow. Our current pedagogy also primes our students to (B) expect that technological "trickledown" from scientific advancement will automatically heal what ails us. Of course, medical science and technology are what we are particularly enamored of. Just consider the preponderance of pharmaceutical ads on prime time TV between the hours of 7:00 and 11:00. How curious that it's now commonplace that drugs and medications--not to mention the plethora of cosmetic enhancements--are pitched to prompt the public to plead with their doctors to prescribe them to heal what ails them. It's like the public is being told to write their own Rx for a doctor to authorize! Never mind the unintended consequences. Of course, they always happen; but, you know, technology's next "advance" will surely address and solve those too.

Today's pedagogy (C) does not make its students particularly ready for old age. Forget the fact that we are enamored of youth and youthfulness, yet know precious little about the real sources of "the fountain of youth." Forget too that, according to some statistics, a majority of seniors are not financially ready to live off their savings long term, having, it seems, only about $600 for emergency expenses in savings. Many seniors basically live from one social security check to the next. The search for wisdom used to be a by-product of our higher education, even if not directly a part of the curriculum. No longer. Gone are the days when even Catholic universities prize theology and philosophy (the "Queen of the sciences") the way they once did even within my lifetime. No, now educational success is pitched and predicated on financial success; but the irony is that the current cost of college exceeds many graduates' ready employment opportunities that are adequate to cover those college costs. Starting a family is postponed because of the cost. Buying a house used to be a readily accessible middle class ideal. What a concept! Being able to afford a home of one's own. Yet how many college graduates are living with their parents and postponing marriage, family and/or a house because they can't afford it?

My main issue (D) with western pedagogy is its imbalance towards discursive thought that rides the wild horse of conceptualization into battles both verbal and physical that it might otherwise rein itself up short from if. If what? If from the early get-go stages, our educational regimen had balanced its emphasis on language skills and conceptual virtuosity with introduction and training to become friendly and familiar with the non-conceptual, non-discursive dimension of mind. Don't have a clue what that is? You've just proved my point.

The dimension of mind we don't recognize and honor and train our students up in is the naturally occurring timeless spacious awareness dimension. It balances the busy, "busyness" dimension by being able to rest content without stressful ambition in a quiet spacious stillness that needs no entertainment to be perfectly content. It doesn't need to be somewhere else instinctively feeling somewhere else is always preferable to the here and now.

This dimension gives the warhorse of the conceptual mind a clear stream and quiet stable to change from charging into battle to policing its own mind in a solitude that is not lonely. It is out of this spacious, timeless dimension that one prepares to be ready to enter any space with a battle readiness that is peacefully aggressive and kindly in its confrontations. It is that "place" where both feet can be planted squarely in mid-air. Where presence doesn't require ego's pre-eminence. Where confrontation can be peacefully aggressive. Why is that possible? Because when the mind has been trained to become friendly and familiar with its own naturally occurring timeless spacious dimension, it has learned how to be wrathful without being angry with nasty negativity. Being able to be wrathful without nasty negative anger has a close relation to tough love, and is a skill from the spiritual technology toolkit of the Buddha. It knows there's wisdom in silent confrontation that let's wise silence do the talking. It's become skilled in silently reflecting back another's foolishness, and letting it confound itself. No words needed. In other words, it has learned to know a reality that exists beyond language capability to corral or capture it in words. It knows what is ineffable. The inconceivable is not beyond its reach and range, and it gives birth to the impregnable with no need to show off its offspring. These are qualities of the wisdom mind that in our eurocentric absorption with technology we either overlook or dismiss with distain. At its best and purest, it teaches a contemplative <u>science</u> [sic], characterized by i) acute observations of internal and external phenomena ii) that give rise to theoretical predictions beyond the conception of physical science and that iii) are experientially and empirically verified in one's own personal experience. Finally iv) they can be repeatedly verified by anyone adequately prepped and made ready to apply the appropriate methodology of mindfulness that gives rise to the entire process in the first place.

This contemplative science arose exclusively in India about 3500 years ago. About 2500 years ago, the Buddha Shatayamuni developed its shamata technology (q.v.) by inventing the vipassana refinement technology, which supplemented shamata. This contemplative <u>science</u> was openly practiced--not hidden in some remote Shangri-la--in Indian universities for a thousand years, 200 years before our first universities in Bologna, Oxford and Paris came into being. But western, eurocentric, colonial arrogance and condescension didn't bother to notice. Well, we're noticing now. Because our foremost physical science, quantum mechanics, has virtually "thrown up its hands" to say, "We don't know the ultimate nature of even physical reality. Does anybody know? We're <u>open</u> and <u>ready</u> to listen."

If this isn't a profound and remarkable cultural "First," I don't know what is. For centuries, western science ironically (?) supported by the Catholic Church's doctrine ("Extra ecclesiam nulla salus est," that is, "outside the Church there is no salvation."), strutted its stuff saying, in effect, about the nonwestern world, "We know and you don't." Well, it turns out quantum mechanics doesn't know. For example, the late renowned quantum physicist, John Wheeler, proved that "space-time," that ultimate container of "real things" has no more than a conventional reality. In effect, it couldn't be proved by strict empirical science to exist as such. At a depth way beyond what can be even conceptually considered "a thing," what these scientists find is something very much like mind, though they are not quite <u>ready</u> to call it that. When pressed to say something, they say something like this: Beyond anything that can be said to exist as a substantial something, there is a potentiality waiting in <u>readiness</u> to respond to "questions" (that is provoked with an experiment of certain kinds) in certain ways." Wait, wait, wait...don't tell me: "readiness to respond if questioned" sounds an awful lot like mind in its naturally occurring timeless spacious dimension! Guess what? Contemplative science from Tibet via India has been saying virtually identical things for 2500 years!

When the Dali Lama hosts his regular five-year interval conferences with the best scientific minds available, the quantum physicists stare slack jawed and amazed that the Dalai Lama can articulate the fundamentals of quantum reality without having any lab equipment at his disposal. How does he know this stuff? The answer: contemplative science.

An indication of our western imbalance in this regard comes to me from a friend whose wife is a very well respected medium. When she gives "readings" at weekend fairs, she may do as many as 50 readings over a two-day period. My friend tells me that out of 100 readings, only two are for men, and only because their wives have dragged them along and into my friend's booth. Wait...wait...before 1900, history clearly writes about how it is the <u>men</u> who <u>led</u> the way, probing spiritual reality for the sake of greater soul depth. What's happened to the men (in the West, at least) in the past 125 years? What's happened is an <u>egregious</u> <u>imbalance</u> in our western pedagogy, let alone our religious institutions' abysmal failure to offer real nurture leading to greater soul depth for the sake of greater spiritual depth.

Once one has become truly friendly and familiar with the naturally occurring timeless and spacious dimension of mind, there is an all-embracing readiness. And why is that? Because one cannot achieve that competence and readiness without having been schooled in a profound discernment process. That process teaches in exquisitely equanimous detail (that is balanced) why the conceptual dimension of mind needs to be balanced by the non-conceptual, otherwise it often acts like a rogue warhorse.

Civility, civil equity, civil equilibrium freed of the hateful perception that our differences are divisive, rather than a source of our democratic strength--these ideals so eloquently stated in the Declaration of Independence--<u>cannot be achieved</u> until and unless we approach our failures to achieve them with open equanimous minds. If the mental tools are imbalanced, the application of those tools will be also. Not maybe. Necessarily. If the ship of state lacks equilibrium and lists because of egregious imbalance, it will never make a safe and secure passage to the Port of Equality. Straightening this boat's deck chairs with geometric precision won't make a damn bit of difference to its sea worthiness. Until a majority of us are prepped with an all-embracing readiness from a balanced mental equanimity, willy-nilly we will continue to be awash with civil discord, civil contentiousness and malicious civil confrontation.